Manipulation Tricks

A Workbook To Help You Master The Techniques In Dark Psychology, Covert Emotional Influence, Mind Control, Nlp & Influencing People With Persuasion Manipulation

Written By

Richard Neel

Table of Contents

INTRODUCTION 7

Power of Words 13

How to use Dark Psychology in Your Daily Life 19

Ways to Protect Yourself from Emotional Manipulation 27

Social Manipulation Strategies 35

Manipulation Techniques to Make your Life Better 45

Recognizing Narcissism 51

Detection And Personality Safety 59

Visual Contact 67

Language And Psychology 77

Creating A Magnetic Presence 81

    Become Sexy 83

The Time To Talk Is Now 87

    Take A Look Around 91

Improving Communication Skills 97

    Body Language 97

    No Fillers 98

    No Cellphones! 98

    Empathy 99

    Language 99

    Eye Contact 100

No Giggling.. 100

Questions... 101

Listening.. 101

Trivia 102

Intentions.. 102

Examples of Hypnotic Language Patterns You Can Use Today! 103

Quantifiers.. 103

Presupposing Social Proof.. 105

Borrowing Authority... 107

Time Clauses 108

Comparative Words 110

Repetitive Words 112

Qualifiers.. 114

CONCLUSION... 115

INTRODUCTION

Thank you for purchasing this book!

In language teaching, elements that find practical uses to learn in general affect students' ways and process information (visual, auditory, or kinesthetic):

1. Deletion.

As students interact with a flood of information, they omit other details to handle the data better.

2. Distortion.

Language students interpret new information in ways that are easy to understand. Although this method is susceptible to errors and misunderstandings, students should formulate their own unique way of learning the lessons.

3. Generalization.

It is also a way to draw broad conclusions from the information at hand, as long as over-generalizations, which result in the misuse of some rules, are handled accordingly.

In addition to techniques that include storytelling, simulation, and role- plays, the following methods for neuro-linguistic programming are currently used freely in various environments of learning:

1. Anchoring.

This method concentrates on an external stimulus or cause, which produces a positive emotional response. Teachers use this technique to create, by introducing keywords or sounds, an anchor that helps students consciously or unconsciously recall the material.

2. Maintaining Flow.

This technique demonstrates that "efficient learning happens when continuously." The instructor develops competitive and collaborative tasks and personalizes them to resolve the knowledge gap and sustain flow according to the personality of the learner.

3. Pacing and Leading.

This technique is a powerful tool for communication and persuasion that uses strategies such as reflection and factualization to create relationships and to encourage students to agree with the teacher.

NLP seems to have a lot of teaching and learning ability. For starters, there are profound implications of the adoption in the education of an underlying cyber epistemology. There are several potential examples of applications of education and training technologies (e.g., Lyall 2002). NLP is widely used to address teaching issues, for example, in the management of classrooms.

In short, an NLP approach for teaching and learning could be described as follows:

- The relationship between teacher and learner is a cybernetic circuit, a dynamic process in which meaning is based on reciprocal feedback, not the exchange of knowledge from one person to another, separate, individual.
- People behave as they perceive and interpret the world, not as 'the country' (i.e., 'the map is not the territory').
- The ways in which people internally represent the world through sensory imagery (including visual, auditory, and kinesthetic) and

language are of primary interest in NLP. NLP is particularly interested in structuring internal

representations both on their own (e.g., position, scale, brightness, etc.) and dynamically (e.g., as sequences). NLP assumes that the internal representational structure displays regularities for each entity and is unique to them.

- NLP also assumes that there are systematic relations between this structure and the language and behavior of the person. Internal perception and understanding of a learner are expressed in their language and external behavior, in different ways (e.g., nonverbal behavior). (NLP courses teach learners to follow these things and to use them).

- All abilities, values, and compartments are acquired (e.g., abilities have corresponding internal sequences, also referred to as 'strategies'). Learning is an accumulation and alteration of these representations and sequences.

- A person's capacity to learn is strongly influenced by his neuro-physiological 'state' (e.g. state of curiosity rather than boredom), and his or her beliefs about learning and about itself as learners (insufficient to learn, and that learning is worthwhile and enjoyable, rather than their opposites). These claims and convictions are often learned and subject to change.

- Such a shift occurs via contact between the instructor and the learner, both consciously and unconsciously, through verbal and non-verbal channels. The functioning that human beings are aware of and can be actively regulated constitutes only a small proportion of their overall functioning.

- All contacts may have a leaning impact. Words and actions of teachers affect learners simultaneously on at least two levels, both their comprehension of the subject in issue (i.e., the complex frameworks of their internal representations) and their world views, including their understanding of learning.

- Therefore, the knowledge of choosing one's own language patterns and behavior as an instructor and responsiveness and interest in their impact and contact with the inner representations of learners is critical to successful teaching and education.

The teaching is basically a cycle of:

1. the development of 'modules' for learning.
2. promoting the discovery of students or strengthening their internal representations.
3. contribute to the desired result or outcome of the background.

Enjoy your reading!

Power of Words

Positive words like peace or love can alter genes' expressions, strengthen our frontal lobe areas, and promote our brain's cognitive functions. They propel the motivational centers of

our minds to have the power to impact us vastly. To understand, we have to go back to what we have learned about how our brain derives meaning from the world around us. We see an image. Out of all the bits of information, we select a specific amount of it to be processed by our brains. This little information in comparison to the information we could have encompasses is chosen based on our profile. After we have this information, we start to assign meaning to those bits of information. We give meaning by comparing the information to our past experiences and knowledge, and once the meaning is derived, the real game starts.

Until the meaning is derived, you have no clue what is going on inside your head. Once the meaning is derived and concluded, our brains start to release certain chemicals or hormones, or neurotransmitters so you can feel the moment and react accordingly. Imagine you see a dog running towards you from a distance. This scene goes to your mind compared to past experiences with dogs, and your brain releases chemicals of fear and hate. Your brains assign these negative words to the scene, "dangerous" or "Lethal," and thus, you would react accordingly.

We can see here how words are playing major roles in our deep psychology, and thus to be able to use them is very important. In this example, if we start to develop the ability to analyze the scenes and assign meanings to them ourselves, we can control our lives. On the other hand, we can persuade other people more effectively and efficiently with the use of words.

Interrogations

There are many techniques used by policemen and investigators based on words alone and show remarkable efficiency. One such method is making the accused say "yes" many times. How does this work? Well, once we say something over and over again, we feel more comfortable saying that. Thus, if you ask a liar a lot of questions that lead to the simple answer of yes, and then ask them about the thing they have done, they might say yes.

It is not 100% effective, but it works. Another method to use yes is by making someone confess to lower crimes first. Ask the accused whether they have ever smoked a cigarette, and if they have, they won't hesitate to say yes to that, but this answer will make them more accustomed to confessing (because most people think of smoking as a taboo). Then ask them if they have ever stolen something in their childhood, how many lies they tell in a day, think about other guilty things they might have committed, and ask them about that. Once you have established these questions, and then ask about the real crime. There is a high possibility they are simply going to confess.

Truism

A truism is a cliché statement and is highly effective when trying to manipulate someone or playing the game of words. Such information may give a solid back-up to your statement. The truism method of manipulation is very simple and is not something related to real Truism. For example, you are debating with someone online about a specific world-history topic. You do what you do, you give nine facts or figures, with sources and references, and the 10th one you give without any citation source and the 10th one is a lie. People are just going to believe you there. That's how people are.

You can build the trust of someone by telling them real things a couple of times, and in the meanwhile, you can feed them some lies, and they are just going to believe that.

When you want to use Truism, there are two starts. Either do your homework on the person you want to feed lies to have the knowledge they have. This would make a great start because you can provide them with the truths or facts you have researched and gain their trust. If you have a vast knowledge of all fields or the areas humans tend to know about, you don't have to do your homework.

Let's take an example. There is a girl in your class who is a somewhat religious conservative type. Now, you want her not to be so because you feel bad for her. If you go and talk to her directly, there is absolutely no way she will let you question her core beliefs. But you can make her question herself.

So, start going to her for a random talk, totally kind and easy. Help her with the homework and stuff. Step one is done. Now do some significant research on her religion and get the loopholes from there. If you are using logic, there are always loopholes in every single possible thing. Even if the scripture is well written, and you don't want to reject the entire religion, you can take out the points where the scripture tells people to be social and meet and greet. Then you can exaggerate that and add a few clauses on your own. Your perfect lie is made. Now you have to implant it in her head.

You tell her many things about her religion because now you have done your research. You talk about history and the obvious things so that she trusts you as a credible source. Once you think it is time, you randomly tell her about your perfect lie. She won't be able to say no because you never lied about any other

16

points, and she would start to question her own beliefs.

You ignited an internal fight and leave her to it, or you can help her along the way. Now let us combine some other things we have learned so far. You mirror and match her and keep her in perfect rapport all the time you spend with her, even if it's 5 minutes barely. This creates an exception for you in her mind, and she would trust your words and you in person. After she is done with her internal fight, be there for

her; tell her more about the religion and various other things. Keep rapport and feed her often lies that lead to your philosophy of life. The game is simple from the moment on. She would start to admire you and trust you. She has an image in mind that you are the person because she became a better version of herself. She would fall in love with you.

Hidden Commands

You would be astonished to see that other than the general methods of manipulation and persuasion, there are also some specific phrases and commands that you can start using the right of the bad to persuade people. Salespeople use these the most.

Weasel Phrases

Tell people how good they'll feel by buying your product or agreeing to your plan.

"Imagine how good you'll feel." Tag Questions
Aren't they, etc. are hard to disagree with, extremely hard for some people. "You won't mind giving me a lift, will you?"

Perhaps not Quite

Tell them you will not advise them to buy your product until they are delighted and have done their research.

Relax

Tell them to relax. The word "relax" has a positive effect and makes someone relaxed and calm. They are likely to listen and agree with you.

Other Words

You can use any word that most people are familiar with and associated with a certain feeling as a command phrase or word.

Just like the word "relax." There are situations where this would not work fine, and in such moments, you can use some other words like calm or peace.

How to use Dark Psychology in Your Daily Life

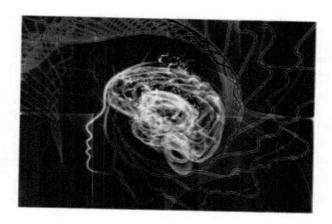

The following are some of the top ten realistic uses for dark psychology in regular life:

Get Prompted

Whether your purpose is to stop smoking, lose weight, or examine a new language, psychology training provides pointers for buying motivated. T

o grow your motivation while drawing close to a project, make use of some of the subsequent tips derived from research in cognitive and educational psychology:

- Introduce new or novel factors to hold your interest high.

- Vary the series to help stave off boredom.

- Study new matters that build on your present understanding.

- Set clear goals that might be at once related to the assignment. Enhance Your Management Abilities

It doesn't count number if you're an office supervisor or a volunteer at a neighborhood teenage activity group.

Having true leadership abilities will, in all likelihood, is vital sometime in the future for your existence.

Not all of us are born leaders, but some easy suggestions from mental studies can improve your leadership capabilities.

One of the research papers looked at three distinct management styles. Primarily based on the findings of this look at and subsequent studies practice several of the following when you are in a management function:

- Offer clear steering but permit group contributors to voice opinions.

- Communicate approximately possible answers to troubles with contributors to the group.

- Focus on stimulating ideas and be inclined to praise creativity. Come To Be a Better Communicator

Conversation involves a whole lot more than just the way you speak or write.

Research indicates that nonverbal indicators make up a big portion of our interpersonal communications.

Some key strategies encompass the subsequent:

- Use proper eye contact.

- Start noticing nonverbal indicators in others

- Use your tone of voice to boost your message. Learn To Better Understand Others

Just like nonverbal communication, your capacity to apprehend your emotions and the feelings of those around you perform an important role in your relationships and professional lifestyles.

The time emotional intelligence refers to your potential to apprehend each of your emotions in addition to those of other human beings.

What can you do to emerge as more emotionally stable? Recall a few of the subsequent techniques:

Cautiously assess your very own emotional reactions. Record your enjoyment and emotions in a journal.

Try to see situations from the angle of a different person. Make Extra Correct Selections

By making use of those techniques for your lifestyles, you can discover ways to make wiser choices. The following time you want to make a huge decision, strive the usage of several the subsequent techniques:

Try using the Six Thinking Hats technique with the aid of searching on from multiple points of view, rational, emotional, intuitive, creative, advantageous, and dark views.

Recall the capacity prices and blessings of choice.

Appoint a grid evaluation approach that offers a score for how a selected decision will fulfill unique requirements you may have.

Enhance Your Reminiscence

Have you ever thought about why you can remember the precise information of childhood events yet forget the call of the new customer you met yesterday? Research on how we form new reminiscences and how and why we forget has caused some of the findings that can be implemented without delay in your daily life. What are some methods you can grow your reminiscence of electricity?

Awareness of the data.

Rehearse what you have discovered. Do away with distractions.
Make wiser financial decisions.

Daniel Kahneman and his colleague Amos Tversky performed a chain of research that looked at how humans manipulate uncertainty and danger while making decisions.

One looks at located that workers could extra than triple their financial savings by making use of some of the following strategies:

Don't procrastinate. Start investing savings now.

Commit earlier to dedicate quantities of your future profits to your retirement financial savings.

Try to be aware of non-public biases that may result in Dark money choices.

Get Higher Grades

The subsequent time you are tempted to whine about pop quizzes, midterms, or finals, consider that research has confirmed that taking checks helps you better consider what you have learned, even if it wasn't on the test.

Every other study discovered that repeated check-taking might be a higher reminiscence aid than studying. College students who were tested repeatedly have been able to remember 61% of the content while the ones within the have a look at group recalled most effective 40%. How can you observe those findings to your lifestyles? While seeking to research new data, self-check frequently to cement what you have learned into your memory.

Become More Effective

Occasionally, it looks as if there are hundreds of books, blogs, and magazine articles telling us the way to get more completed in an afternoon. However, how much of this advice is based on real studies? For example, think about the variety of times you have ever heard that multitasking can help you become more productive.

Studies have discovered that trying to carry out multiple missions at the same time severely impairs pace, accuracy, and productiveness.

What classes from psychology can you operate to boom your productivity? Consider several of the following:

Avoid multitasking while running on complex or dangerous obligations.

Cognizance at the venture at hand Eliminate distractions
Be Healthier

Psychology also can be a useful device for improving your ordinary health. From approaches to encourage workout and better nutrients to new remedies for melancholy, the sector of fitness psychology gives a wealth of beneficial strategies that can help you to be more healthy and happier.

Some examples that you may practice at once in your very own existence:

Research has shown that both daylight and synthetic mild can reduce the symptoms of seasonal affective sickness.

Studies have demonstrated that exercise can contribute to more mental well-being.

Studies have determined that supporting people apprehend the dangers of bad behaviors can lead to healthier choices.

Ways to Protect Yourself from Emotional Manipulation

There will always be people trying to shake your trust-people trying to instill self-doubt inside you. Such people would do their utmost to trick you into thinking that their beliefs are

objective.

Manipulative people are not preoccupied with your needs. They worry about their interests. Once you allow manipulative people in your life, it can be tough to get rid of them. The trick is to have enough self- control to send the boot to dishonest people as soon as you see them. Here are a few ways to get rid of manipulative people from your life:

Don't Fall Into Their Trap.

Most of us come across instances where others seek to manipulate our thoughts, attitudes, or actions and take advantage of them to their benefit. In one such case, you fail to understand the real motive. The person mentally dominates you, and you step into the pit. This emotional abuse often costs you a lot when you make some critical decisions under another person's control, and when it is too late, you know it later.

You have to be conscious when a relationship sounds too good to be true. They are showering you with compassion, gratitude, admiration, congratulations, and affection. You feel like you live in a dream where everything seems perfect. They don't give you a reason to worry. You cannot find any flaws in them. Also, if anything goes wrong, they can begin to weep or feel sorry. You can have become the object of extreme intimacy and feel a passion for the fairy tale.

Individuals often succeed in manipulating their victims after intermittent reinforcement. We can avoid behaving in the same way while fighting back or demanding an answer. The explanation is that they are taking complete care of you now, so they say goodbye to the intermittent strengthening. We no longer need it. Manipulators have different faces, and they can use many ways to get things done. The person may make an undertaking and later deny that you begin to doubt your perception. They do make you feel bad when you try hard to make them aware of their promise. They can employ shallow sympathy and burst into crocodile tears. Eventually, you end up trusting them and even doubting whether you listened correctly.

Steer straight wherever possible

A manipulator's actions typically vary according to the situation they're in. For instance, a manipulator may speak rudely to one person and act respectfully towards another the next moment. When you see these extremes frequently in a person, it would be advisable to stay away from them. And you have to communicate with this guy. That will prevent you from becoming a deceptive victim.

One way to identify a manipulator is to see if a person behaves differently and before other people with different faces. Although we all have a degree of this sort of social distinction, some psychological manipulators seem to dwell in extremes habitually, being highly polite to one person and gross to another-or helpless at one moment, and fiercely violent at another. If you frequently experience this form of behavior from an adult, keep a healthy distance away, and avoid interacting with the person unless you have to. As described earlier, there are nuanced and deep-seated causes for persistent psychological abuse. Saving or saving these is not your job.

There are some circumstances in which you can't entirely leave a relationship-most, usually whether that person is a parent or an extended family member. You probably cannot go cold turkey unless the individual causes serious harm or psychological damage. You need to accept this person completely for who they are and change your relationship standards accordingly. If they were someone you needed validation from before, you would have to quit looking for their validation. Recognize that their advice is not something you need in your life if they were someone you received advice from. When they keep offering it, you can thank them for it and then politely dump it. When setting these limits, be as discreet as you can, and do not tell the other person you are setting them. Creating this shift at your end will take some time, and when you get upset with the other person in the process, you will have to deal with their reaction on top of that.

Call them out on their actions.

Manipulators are always difficult to deal with, but the worst is discreet manipulators. They will stay cool as a cucumber when confronted, and yet rigid and unbending. You may start to get frustrated when you start seeing their faulty reasoning. When you keep fighting with them, you'll find it hard not to raise your voice a bit. You're going to start looking like the irrational one, and they're going to try to take back control in remaining calm, based on their "maturity."

Defending yourself is tempting and trying to get the other person to see what is going on. But a true manipulator will not change their tune, and the more you give in to that urge to protect yourself, the more they will twist your words more. Suppose you are in a situation with a true manipulator. In that case, the two goals for any conflict that are taking place should be to resolve and leave, whether leaving the current conversation or exiting the relationship. Evite threats, accusations, lose patience, accuse the other person of coercion, or become excessively emotional. Stick to honest, factual, and respectful declarations when you speak.

Some things require a high degree of intelligence, flexibility, or self- discipline when dealing with a manipulative person. You might not have the self-control to react without losing your temper and making things worse. If that's the case, accept this about yourself and take extra steps to avoid a tense confrontation (invite a mediator into the conversation, for example, or send an email instead of meeting in person, so you have time to think through what you say).

Touch Their Centre of Gravity

Manipulative people actively take advantage of their tactics against you. Through your enemies, they will become enemies and turn them against you. They're going to dangle some small reward in front of you and make you chase it relentlessly- they're going to take it away any time you get close to it. You will forever keep past acts above your head. And on and on. Avoid letting those who exploit you use their tactics against you. Switch the tables in, instead. Build your plan and hit them where it hurts. When you are forced to deal with a dishonest person who, no matter how hard you try to avoid them, tries to make your life miserable, you have only one choice, find their center of gravity and destroy it. This center may be associates, followers, or subordinates to the deceptive individual. It may be a high-level talent or advanced knowledge of a particular area. They can manage it as a particular resource.

Figure out what their center of gravity is and make it yours anyway. Creating alliances with those close to them, hiring people to replace them with their skillsets and knowledge base, or siphoning away their precious assets. This will throw them off balance and push them to concentrate on managing their life, not yours.

Believe in your decision.

Many people are going around asking for the views of other people on anything. How do I want to do with my life? What am I fantastic at? Where am I, then? Avoid searching for other people so you can describe yourself. Define yourself. Believe in yourself. What distinguishes winners from losers is not the ability to listen to other people's opinions; it's the ability to listen to one's own opinions. You prevent dishonest people from influencing your life by setting up your

values and keeping them tightly onto them. This will serve as a firewall to your convictions, keeping manipulators ostracized and out of your way.

Try not to fit right in.

Keep reinventing yourself. One myth is the belief that continuity is somehow admirable or related to achievement. Manipulative people want you to be consistent so that they can count on you to advance their agendas. They want you to show up at 9 am every day and work at minimum wage for them.

Consistent assembly lines. The prison is uniform. Consistency is how they trap you in a shell. It's their way of manipulating you. The only way to stop being exploited is by consciously going against all the barriers other people seek to create for you. Hold on, trying to blend in. Instead, they're looking to stand out. Act to be different in some way, and never remain the same for too long. By design, personal growth needs a lack of consistency. Constant change is expected-constant reinvention.

Never ask for permission.

We have been trained to ask for permission constantly. As a boy, we had to ask for everything we wanted — to be fed, changed, and burped. We had to get permission to go to the bathroom during the day, and we had to wait to eat lunch at a designated time and wait for our turn to play with toys. As a result, most people never cease to expect permission.

Employees around the world are waiting for a promotion and waiting for their turn to talk. Most are so used to being chosen that they sit in meetings in silence, afraid to talk out of turn or even lift their hands. It's a different way of living.

Build a greater sense of mission

Destiny driven people aren't easily fooled. The reason manipulators in this world tend to prosper is that so many people lead a purposeless life. They're going to do anything. Because, somehow, nothing matters. People who lack intent waste time. There is no rhyme or explanation behind how they live their lives. We don't know where to go or why they are here. So, to avoid going insane, they're working in meaningless jobs and stuffing their minds full of celebrity gossip, reality television, and other useless types of media. They remain busy to avoid the desperate feeling of emptiness growing inside them. This profession and loneliness empower deceptive individuals.

Social Manipulation Strategies

Here are some of the most powerful strategies for manipulating people in social or public settings and scenarios.

Cash In On the Home Court

You ever noticed why several network marketing professionals always insist that you come to their home or office for a presentation rather than giving you a presentation in your home? There is a simple manipulation strategy behind it. When you negotiate within a physical space that belongs to you, you are subconsciously in a more authoritative position.

You have more influence, control, power, and dominance when you are in a physical space that is your domain. It reflects in your body language, attitude, words, and actions. The place can be anywhere from your home to office to car, which you are comfortable and familiar with. Network marketers are always attempting to cash in on the home-court advantage, which is why they will insist that you come over for a presentation to their place.

When you sign an important deal or negotiate terms of a critical association, always persuade the other party to come over to your office or home for a talk. The comfort and familiarity of your space will put you in a position of greater confidence and authority, thus increasing your chances of cracking the deal in your favor.

Tell people that they need to understand the process, or you need to explain everything to them in detail, which is why they should come over to your place. This is the angle you present to them. The reality is

that you are giving yourself a higher position by conducting negotiations in a space that you own and are therefore familiar and comfortable in.

Distraction Strategy

This is one of the most common manipulation techniques used by governments, political parties, world leaders, politicians, and other public personalities to divert the public attention from vital problems by introducing continuous distractions and trivial/unimportant information.

This way, the public attention remains fixated on minor issues while the real political and social problems are hidden under the carpet. It gives the illusion of being busy with something, though that something is of little consequence in their life. They don't have the time to think about the negative impact of essential issues in their lives and their leaders' inability to resolve these issues.

Create Problems That Don't Exist and Offer Solutions

This is another classic social manipulation strategy that is widely used throughout the world. It consists of creating an image or foreseen issue to stimulate a specific reaction among victims of manipulation or the public. Then, the manipulator carefully introduces a solution to become the ultimate messiah.

For example, they are allowing urban violence to build and thrive initially or supporting terrorist camps. This can be followed by making people aware of how their security is the government's prime concern and how leaders will go all out to intensify security measures to ensure public safety.

You present a problem and offer a solution without letting the victims realize that you were directly responsible for creating the problems. This way, you become the solution provider who can get people to act in a desired manner.

The Painful Reality

Your boss urges everyone at the workplace to put in additional hours of work or work during weekends. He/she may lead you to believe that you all stand to lose your jobs, and the market is tight, which means that you have to step up and go the extra mile to survive. They will inform you about how other companies who weren't able to bag big projects couldn't sustain operation costs and eventually closed down.

The managers will convince you about how a few sacrifices from your side can go a long way in saving the company's fortunes. They are projecting their decision as painful yet necessary. They'll tell how they don't want you to stay late at work, but there's no other option, or the company has to stay afloat. A majority will resign to the idea of working late.

To Project Victims as Ignorant or Stupid

One way to get people to do what you want them to do publicly, professionally, or socially is to make them feel how ignorant or stupid they or how they don't understand something. For instance, if you are looking to introduce new technology that will save labor costs and increase profits, it may have many people rebelling against it for fear of losing their jobs.

Using the ignorant manipulation tactic, you inform people about how they cannot comprehend technology, which is designed to make things easier. You are playing on their lack of awareness or uncertainty about a thing.

You are replacing revolt with guilt by making the victims feel responsible for their unfortunate situation or lack of intelligence/capabilities. Thus, instead of rebelling, workers blame or devaluate themselves, thus inhibiting further action.

Foot in the Door Strategy

This technique comes first to the times of door-to-door salespersons. To prevent people from shutting their doors on their faces, salespersons use to put their foot in the door and request a couple of minutes to speak to the homeowners.

Once they got those 2-3 minutes with the homeowners, they would build upon it and try to sell their products to them.

This is one of the most effective manipulation techniques in a social or public setting because it gives you that tiny opening, which you can cleverly encase on. You attempt to break the ice by making a small request from the other person they generally won't refuse. The actual or bigger request follows this what you are doing by asking for a smaller request to be fulfilled in putting you gently in the door and triggering a series of positive replies.

Once a person agrees to a small request, it is challenging to follow it with a refusal. The trick here is to request for something tiny and reasonable that the victim can easily fulfill. This is to be followed by the actual intended or larger request.

Drown Them with Facts, Information, and Statistics

Emotional manipulation doesn't work on everyone, especially in social and professional settings. Here, people are more inclined to follow the logic and rational arguments. Drown these folks in information by quoting research, facts, figures, statistics, and more.

Have numbers ready on your fingertips for any objections and clarifications. Overwhelm people with statistics, logical arguments, and research. Be armed with the vital information to "intellectually bully" people. Present yourself as the ultimate authority or the source of knowledge in a particular field. Take advantage of established expertise to the fullest.

One way to manipulate people with logic is to present research, statistics, and figures in a compelling and imposing manner. Focus on areas where you believe they may not have sound knowledge and question them about it. This establishes their weakness in their own eyes. They will realize that they have little or no information about this area and that you are more experienced or knowledgeable than them.

This technique works well during business negotiations, sales, social debates, and other social or public settings.

You gain a smart subconscious edge over the other person, making them more defenseless and open to listening to you. It creates a sort of intellectual superiority, making them feel inadequate and compels them to comply with your demands.

The Victim Talks First

When you get another party to agree to your negotiation terms or buy from you, allow them to talk first. This allows you as a persuader, influencer, or manipulator to establish their baseline. What are their strengths and weaknesses? What are their thoughts, emotions, fears, and behavior patterns? Are they more hesitant or self-confident? Do they appear extroverted/open or introverted/closed? Are they approaching the deal or sales with an element of hesitation? Are they overwhelmed by your presence? How does their body language reveal about them?

Allowing them to communicate first helps you set a baseline for their strengths and weaknesses, which can be utilized to get them to act in the desired direction. You can also prepare a list of questions that you can ask them to establish a baseline. The idea is to get them thinking in the direction of taking action in your favor. For instance, if you plan to sell insurance, you ask them a list of questions that help you establish their fears and therefore allow you to play on these fears for getting them to sign up quickly.

Kill Trust Issues by Sharing Something Personal

Many people are wary of being manipulated because they've been misled or manipulated in the past. They come with a baggage of trust issues and always operate with a hint of suspicion. Such people are potentially difficult to manipulate since they always have their guard on.

However, one way to overcome trust issues or help them drop their guard is by sharing personal information. This makes them lower the walls and increase their trust in you. Ensure that the information you share is confidential or personal enough to break the trust barrier. The information you share may be real or fabricated. However, the other person must believe it.

Be a Master at Debates and Public Speaking

It is about being able to persuade or influence people into taking the desired action. If you want to develop your persuasion or people- convincing skills, sign up for a public speaking class. You will learn to put across a gripping, impactful, and assertive manner without getting aggressive or pushy.

Notice how some of the best public speakers orators can hypnotically charm people with their verbal and nonverbal communication skills. They use everything from their words to gestures to posture to voice tone to persuade people to think or act like them. Convincing people takes a confident and powerful persona.

When you portray a confident and imposing personality, people automatically sit up and pay attention to what you say. Attract people like magnets by learning powerful strategies for appearing more convincing and presenting ideas in a more attention- grabbing/spellbinding manner.

You can use the right environment at the right time to ask for someone to do something for you. Debunk the theory that there are a place and time for everything and make the environment work in your favor.

For instance, if you are partying with a boss or coworker on a Friday night, instead of waiting until Monday morning to ask them for a favor, use the relaxed setting of a pub or bar. They'll be less guarded, more chilled out and relaxed, and in a more positive mood. Your chances of getting them to agree to the favor may be higher in a more relaxed setting where they don't expect you to ask for such a favor. Change the setting where you'd normally ask something like this to increase your chances of getting people to agree.

44

Manipulation Techniques to Make your Life Better

Have you ever noticed that the most successful people are also the most persuasive? In the workplace, it is rarely the aggressive bossy people that rise to the top. Great leaders

have a knack for making other people feel better about themselves and achieve better results. Use the following techniques to become a better manipulator both at work and at home.

Inspire confidence

Do you give compliments regularly? Are you quick to praise people when they achieve their goals? If not, then why not? Make sure you tell people when they have done an excellent job and encourage them to greater things.

Once you master this technique and feel comfortable giving praise, this will spill over into your personal life. If your partner looks sensational, then tell them! If your kids have done well at school, then reward them with your praise.

Only give sincere compliments and do not use them to play people. If you are using manipulation to avoid tasks at work, you will soon get a reputation for using people.

Repetition

Many people believe that passion alone can make an idea stand out amid a sea of other ideas. This is not true and successful people realize that the key to standing out in society's information overload is repetition. We have all developed filters to protect us from the

bombardment of information in this media-led world and need to hear something multiple times before it sinks in. If you have a great idea and voice it to someone, make sure you follow up with a written version.

Deliver your message in context

Often, we are tempted to make ourselves look more intelligent by using technical jargon or abstract references. You can achieve better results if you tune into your audience's frame of mind. Avoid non- specific terms. If you know how to make things "easier to use" or "better and quicker," then state how much easier or how much better and quicker.

Personalize your message

Statements of fact can often be bland and uninteresting. If you can personalize your speech, you have a greater impact on your audience. This is a great tool at work when approaching someone creative, and then tailor your speech to reflect this. This technique will also help your social life. Whenever you meet new people, try and do a bit of homework to know more about them.

Use your contacts

Everyone is more open to people who they believe have mutual associations. Your connections can help you progress and providing you don't abuse their influence can aid your progress at work. Your credibility can rise with the relevance of your contacts and friends.

Use visualization techniques

Have you noticed that the most successful sales pitches have a strong visual element? Picture Apples Steve Jobs and you can visualize the stage and the graphics that he used to get his message across. Even his clothes became part of the whole message that Apple was trying to convey. Not everyone will comprehend what you see in your mind's eye, especially if they have less knowledge in the domain you represent.

Social media

The potential to reach thousands of people who can help you in your career is invaluable.

Potential investors or customers are all waiting for you to tell your story or promote your product. Social media allows you to solicit ideas from a huge audience, all with the click of a mouse. The power of a "like button" is not to be ignored! The evidence of thousands of positive affirmations will only serve to amplify your voice and make more people listen.

Your social life can also thrive online. Groups of like-minded people are all out there waiting for you to join them. Maybe you have a passion for sailing or extreme sports but aren't sure of the facilities near you. Facebook is a place to start looking for groups in your area, reach out, and connect. Use Twitter and Integra to help your dating life if you are looking for love! Providing you take precautions and always meet for the first time in public you can meet some interesting people!

Social media can also be a brutal place, and you must monitor your settings. Before you join a group, make sure they can only see the information you are comfortable with.

Listen intently

Adopt a relaxed posture and allow them to tell you all about themselves. Show genuine interest and ask pertinent questions as you listen.

What is the common factor all these questions have? "That is fascinating. How did you manage that?" "Interesting. Do you have any examples?"

"Your knowledge about……. Is amazing, what do you think about…?"

They are all questions that elicit a response. This shows the speaker that you are not just listening, but you have a genuine interest in what they say. You also allow the speaker to expand the conversation, which creates a bond between the two of you.

Persuasion and manipulation are both powerful forces that can be used to make your life better. Ethical communications help others and make them a part of your team.

Recognizing Narcissism

In popular culture, narcissism, usually referring to vanity and self- absorption, is thrown quite loosely. It reduces narcissism to a common quality that everyone possesses and downplays the actual disorder's signs. While narcissism does appear on a continuum, it is very different from narcissism as a full-fledged personality disorder.

People who fit the Narcissistic Personality Disorder behave in an overly manipulative way in the context of romantic relationships owing to their deceitfulness, lack of sensitivity, and propensity to be interpersonally exploitative.

In any relationship, we must learn to identify red flags while engaging with others who show malignant narcissism or antisocial behaviors to better protect ourselves from exploitation and violence, establish appropriate boundaries with others, and make educated choices on which we have in our life. Knowing the essence of these toxic interactions and how they affect us has a huge impact on our capacity to care for ourselves.

What is Narcissistic Abuse?

Narcissistic partners often engage in chronic manipulation and devaluation of their victims, leaving the offenders to feel worthless, anxious, and even suicidal. Such a form of continuous coercion involves a cycle of idealization-devaluation-dump violence in which they "love bomb" their partners, devalue them, and discard them before the trauma starts again. This is defined as narcissistic abuse – harassment from an NPD partner or the other end of the narcissistic continuum. This form of violence can leave permanent psychological and emotional scars.

Narcissists will subject you to a dizzying cocktail of traumatic highs and lows in an attempt to get you hooked to the drug they abuse. This is so subtle that many people don't realize they've been abused – others identify the techniques ten years into a marriage with a coercive abuser. At the same time, some are lucky enough to discover it early in the relationship.

In narcissistic abuse, toxic behaviors can involve but are not limited to:

Being overly critical and controlling toward their partners and condemning them covertly and overtly by cruel verbal abuse and manipulative behaviors only isolate them.

This can include name-calling, harsh insults veiled as laughs, demeaning, and contemptuous remarks about the victim's appearance, intelligence, and line of work, lifestyle, and sets of expertise, accomplishments, or other networks of help outside the relationship.

Being abusive, physically, or sexually. This may involve hitting the person with objects, punching, shoving, slapping, choking, or pushing the victim, pressuring the victim to have sex without consent, and coercing the victim into sexual situations in which they are not at peace. In some way, they may threaten to leave the victim or ruin the life of the victim if they fail to fulfill their wishes.

They are manufacturing hostile or aggressive situations where the victim is led to emotional distress, particularly by the abuser's narcissistic rage of the abuser over seemingly insignificant or irrelevant items. The abuser creates an atmosphere in which the victim feels trapped, controlled, and limited to what they may do or do.

Engaging in hot and cold behavior that quickly switches between a loving and abusive person. This is a cycle of abuse called "idealization, devaluation, and discard." This involves punishing the person with no apparent reason, cold and callously, only to revert to tender, affectionate conduct in a periodic reinforcement strategy. It will require the victim to anticipate less every time they interact and train

them to equate love with unpredictability, anxiety, and uneasiness. The survivor is then humiliated in a demeaning way, often followed by a smear campaign so that the narcissist thinks they have "won" the breakup.

Controlling every aspect of their partner's life to the point of separating them from family and friends; this involves sabotaging the interests of the victim, family relationships, important things in life, or their goals and aspirations.

Stonewalling their victims in silence should raise any concerns about the relationship. Subjecting the victim to silent treatments and disappearances during the abuse process to build a feeling of chronic insecurity inside the victim, causing the victim to walk on eggshells and through their attempts to appease their abusive spouse.

Triangulating their victims with other love interests and their ex- partners, engaging in pathological lying and deceit while pursuing numerous outsides of relationship affairs; comparing the victim to others for their looks, temperament, performance, and other qualities to instill a feeling of worthlessness inside them. This infidelity is not motivated by the main partner's frustration but by a sadistic desire for narcissistic resources. This supply occurs in the shape of several people's attention and the mental pain from the victim in response to the triangulation.

By denying, minimizing, or rationalizing the abuse, massacring their spouses into thinking the violence is not real. That involves deflecting all responsibility talks through circular debates and word salad to not be kept responsible for their behavior.

They are subjecting their victim to smear campaigns to damage their image and reputation so that the survivor of violence is left with no help network. It includes projecting their abusive behavior into the victim, and one trusts in their abuse accounts.

While using a false charismatic self to make their victims appear like the "crazy" ones, they accuse and project their malignant traits into their partners during conversations. It's almost as though they pass down their traits and flaws to their victims as though they were suggesting, "Take my pathology here. I don't like that." That's what narcissistic abuse feels like – and sadly, no psychology class or diagnostic manual teaches the full scope of narcissistic abuse. Manipulative techniques can be found in numerous books from narcissism experts, stories by behavioral health providers that have worked with survivors as clients, and survivor accounts.

It is the malignant behaviors of a narcissist, and how they affect us is the key to understanding that the spouse is a narcissist. Regardless of your gender or background, anyone can be a target of narcissistic violence. A narcissistic abuser may end in survivors becoming sad, suicidal, anxious, constantly on alert, and useless. If the mate displays certain types of toxic habits, they are physically, mentally, and psychologically abusive at the very least. While malignant narcissists are certainly very risky, partners who show only any of these traits and refuse to change don't need NPD diagnosis to allow victims to realize that they have a toxic relationship partner.

What Causes Narcissism?

The Narcissus myth is a common one to describe the ego and self-absorption of a narcissist. Still, there is a lack of deeper discussion about the nature of the full-fledged personality condition. Narcissism is growing in our society, but how exactly does it manifest, especially as a personality disorder? There are many theories of how narcissism arises in an adult — from a "narcissistic burn" in infancy to a parent's history of idealization and devaluation. It is also a neural point of view that reflects mainly whether a narcissist's brain has compassion-related structural abnormalities.

Some theories say that narcissism may be created by the child's overvaluation, causing the child to stay like a child forever for its presumed perfection without any repercussions or a basis in empirical fact. A trend of overvaluation rather than devaluation by a parent might have driven a child to aborted emotional development – that is to say, a child who is abused to the extent that they grow an unhealthy sense of superiority and disdain for others' emotions.

Narcissists can probably be produced in several ways and can come from various backgrounds; an interaction between biology and the environment may generate their narcissism.

Detection And Personality Safety

In addition, we are going to try and make it easier for you to spot manipulation. When you have a good idea of what is going on with the people around you and we mean truly knowing what they're planning it can help to keep you safer in a lot of situations. We will look over how to be exceptionally mindful in what you do on a daily basis and ways that you can build your self-esteem. When you are trying to understand human behavior it's important to understand yourself. Looking at your verbal and nonverbal skills can allow you better insight as to what other people are thinking because you won't understand how their bodies work as compared to your own.

Trying to figure out when somebody is taking advantage of you can be difficult. There are absolutely signs that you can watch out for. In fact, there are a lot of different great articles surrounding the thoughts of if somebody is or is not trying to take advantage of you. With the ability to see when somebody's intentions are less than pure you will keep yourself better protected and in turn, lead a happier life. It can be very frustrating when you're uncertain of someone's intentions and even worse when you find out they were simply around to take advantage of you.

People are pretty crafty, and they will use your emotions against you. Some people love to feign confusion. You may have made it very clear what your expectations are, and they simply pretend that they don't understand. If it is somebody that you know fairly well it can be easy to see that they are trying to take advantage of you because you may know that they're quite smart and usually catch on to things quickly.

However, if you're dealing with somebody you don't know very well you may just assume that they're not very intelligent and need a lot of direction to get something done. They're active confusion can be frustrating and leave you dealing with whatever it was you asked of them.

In a relationship, feigning confusion can be horribly detrimental. Let's say that you know your girlfriend or boyfriend is cheating on you, but they simply play dumb. You may not have exact proof and in their ability to act confused or non-understanding of what you are saying can leave you two sticking with a detrimental situation. Pay close attention to the person you are dealing with so that you can have a good understanding of whether or not they actually have the capacity to get what you are saying.

Some also really like to play the victim. You've probably met a person or two in your life that does this. Everything that is going on with them is simply terrible. They do this so that they can have your attention and get you to do what they want. Sympathy is a powerful feeling. If somebody is working through a hardship, naturally, good people want to help them. Somebody with malicious intent will use this to their advantage. Knowing that you are a good person or realizing that you help people around you can encourage them to play the part of the victim to gain your trust and sympathy. People that play the victim tend to do it in their everyday lives. Each person that they come into contact with they have another sob story to make them feel bad. If you are around somebody that has a generally negative attitude this could be because they like to play the victim. Some people do it unconsciously, but others do it to get you under their thumb. Be careful when you're handing out sympathy and empathy for those around you and make sure that they deserve it.

In today's world we hear a lot about shaming. This can be done in a variety of ways and it is insanely detrimental. It can start out with little

digs about the way you look, feel, or. It may be that you did not do something up to the standard of the person speaking to you. In the real world, they are simply doing this to get you under their thumb. When people give us critiques it can be difficult to understand that they may not be true. Human beings, naturally, take things to Heart. Shame is a very powerful feeling that can tear you down quickly. Once you start feeling ashamed of yourself and one way or another it is difficult to pull yourself out of it. So recognizing when somebody is simply trying to shame you into submission is important for your mental health.

Using shame does not necessarily always making digs. If you have met a very sarcastic person, they could be using their sarcasm to make you feel ashamed. This type of behavior is unacceptable, and it should be acknowledged from the very beginning. There is a time and a place for sarcasm but when it is making you feel terrible about yourself you need to put a stop to it right away. Otherwise, you may be given control of yourself and your life to somebody else.

Divert Attention

When people are trying to take advantage of you, they may use diversion techniques. By throwing you off of a certain thought or path they can easily change the subject and get the eyes off of them. Being aware and staying on track of what you were saying is important. This goes hand-in-hand with knowing what you're going to say and spending the time to think before you speak. With clear concise thoughts you won't have to worry about people trying to divert your attention away from them.

When people try to divert attention often, they are trying to pass the blame on to somebody else. This is a very dangerous game and can end up pitting you against a friend, co-worker, or family member. So, as noted it's extremely important to have your thoughts collected

before entering into any sort of serious conversation. It truly can help to ensure that you do not get taken advantage of by those that are skilled and diversion techniques.

Some people will do their very best to make you feel guilty in order to be able to take advantage of you. This commonly happens with people that know you better than others. When those around you are aware of the fact that you strive to be a good person it can, absolutely, be used against you. There is nothing wrong with wanting to be a good person, but it does tends to make people feel more guilty when they've done something wrong.

Everyone has moments in time where they're not the best person and that's okay. Accepting the fact that everyone makes mistakes can help to ensure that those around you cannot use guilt to control you. Sure, most of us want to make good decisions and do the right thing by not only ourselves but those that are around us. Knowing that this is not always the case and we all have screw-ups is very helpful. Guilt is a common denominator and taking control over somebody or using them to your advantage.

Denial

Denial is another component that people frequently used to take advantage of others. If you don't have hard evidence against somebody what is to stop them from simply saying no I didn't do that. It then comes down to your word against theirs. If somebody is vehemently denying what you are saying eventually you start to believe it. You may question the information and where you got it. This can cause distrust among those that you trust the most. Denial is dangerous especially when you trust your sources. Hearsay is a difficult thing to prove, however, it can be very detrimental to someone's psyche. As you start to doubt whether or not your accusations are true you may also start to doubt other things in your life. This allows control to the person

that is making all of the denials. They can pray on this to try and bend you to their well. In addition, once they have made you accept the fact that their denial is true they might start looking for favors.

Neuro-linguistic programming skills can really help in this department. Most people that are quick to deny something have some facial movements or body movements to give them away. When you start to study these techniques, it can be much more simple to figure out who is riding the denial train. When you understand that somebody is simply denying the accusations to save face or keep them self out of trouble it becomes easier to figure it out and understand that is what's going on.

Lie

Liars are all around us. From the time we are little there are lies in our lives. Ones that we have told and ones that others have told us. Liars are, typically, trying to take advantage of you. Sometimes the lie that is told is quite harmless and can be brushed off. Other times, they are major lies that can ruin lives.

We talked a bit about lying earlier and when it comes down to it every person in the world tells a lie on occasion. When we tell a lie with good intent it doesn't make it much better than align with mal intent, but it is more understandable. Sometimes it is simply easier to tell a white lie than it is to hurt somebody's feelings or cause turmoil for somebody that you care about.

Then there are the other types of Lies, the big ones. These can affect not only your daily life and relationships but also your job. When people are telling a lot late and lies it can be very difficult to deal with. Emotions may become heightened, especially, if you know for a fact that they are lying. This can make you act out in a way that you normally would not.

Obviously, if you're at work and you have a major meltdown because somebody thought you trusted is telling a major lie it's going to lead to trouble. Spotting Liars can be difficult so be careful who you decide to put your full trust into.

Visual Contact

In this chapter, we are going to be taking an in-depth looking into visual contact. This chapter aims to give you additional resources and insights into the way visual contact can help you get the

upper hand in your daily interactions.

Thus far, we have touched on the subject of visual contact on several occasions. We have focused on what eye contact, or lack thereof, might be conveying. Indeed, visual contact is one of the core skills which master communicators dominate.

Visual contact is all about establishing communication in such a way that your eyes reinforce your message. As such, your eyes will drive home what you mean to say and not send mixed messages. Unfortunately, most folks don't realize this. So, they soon find that their eyes end up betraying their true intentions. That is how important eye contact can be. Nevertheless, one of the most important functions that eye contact serves is rapport. When you meet someone for the first time, effective eye contact can establish immediate rapport. What effective eye contact signals to your interlocutor is that you are genuine and sincere. When you are able to drive this message home, you will instantly become liked and accepted by those around you.

On the other hand, ineffective eye contact will lead others to doubt your true intentions and dismiss you as someone who is not trustworthy. Failure to establish effective rapport can easily derail your endeavors. Consequently, avoiding ineffective eye contact is paramount to your success.

Throughout this book, we have referred to effective and ineffective eye contact. Yet, you might be asking yourself how you can specifically achieve effective visual contact while avoid ineffective visual contact. So, let's take a look at specific aspects to both sides of the equation. First of all, effective eye contact conveys sincerity in your message. When your eye contact is congruent with your words, you will be regarded as an effective communicator. This can be achieved by genuinely meaning what you say. It is really that simple. You see, when a person is lying, there is an instinctive response inside of them that triggers the brain to enter into a defensive state. After all, what can you do if you get caught in a lie? In such cases, you need to assume a defensive posture in order to protect yourself from potential scrutiny and attacks.

Do you see where we are going with this?

Lying triggers the same response from the brain as if the individual fears they are going to be attacked. Lying places an individual in a vulnerable position. This vulnerability is directly proportional to the ability that said individual may have to defend themselves. So, if the liar feels confident that they have constructed an effective lie, they will be able to act much more naturally. In contrast, if the individual feels they don't have a solid lie, they will feel threatened and vulnerable.

That being said, liars can be easy to spot based on eye contact alone.

The first, and most obvious sign is evasive eye contact. But it is not enough to dismiss a person a liar simply because they are reluctant to match your gaze. As we have indicated before, there is the possibility that your interlocutor is simply a shy person. Thus, they feel uncomfortable exchanging looks and glances with the folks they communicate with.

Since evasive eye contact is insufficient grounds to dismiss someone as a liar, it is important to focus specifically on what your counterpart's eyes are actually doing and saying.

One important thing to look out for is too much eye contact. If you see that your interlocutor is far too insistent on staring at you directly in the eyes, you may have a liar on your hands. The reasoning behind this is that since evasive eye contact signals a potential lie, then the opposite would indicate sincerity. However, too much eye contact signals someone who is trying too hard. As such, this is a telltale sign of suspicious behavior.

In addition, a person who is lying may try to intimidate through visual contact. This tactic is widely used by professional liars. That way, you will feel compelled to accept (though not necessarily believe) what they are saying as successful intimidation will get you to back off and not ask any questions.

So, what can you do in such a situation?

You can diffuse the situation by avoiding a staring contest. If you choose to engage in a staring contest, be prepared to go face to face with a potentially aggressive person. So, you can diffuse the situation by asking a sharp question during a brief moment of matching gazes.

A good example of this is police interrogation. You can take cues from police detectives on television. Often, when they interrogate a suspect, they ask sharp questions while staring at them directly in the eyes. Then, they back off and let the suspect enough slack to answer the question. Most of the time, suspects will stick to their lie except that they won't be as convincing.

Another important layer to visual contact has to do with blinking.

Blinking is an involuntary movement that helps protect they eyes from dust and dirt in the air. Also, it helps keep eyes fresh and avoid them from getting too dry. So, blinking is an important bodily function that we all engage in. Now, a normal blinking rate can be something like 10 times per minute. This depends on the circumstances of course. In some cases, you might be so carried away by something you are watching that you might forget to blink. In other cases, you might simply be inattentive. In that case, you may simply blink at a lower rate due to your reduced alertness.

That is why too much blinking conveys the opposite message.
When a person is in a stressful situation, their heart rate and pulse will begin to

climb. This alters other involuntary movements including blinking. So, it is almost unavoidable that anyone who is nervous, anxious or perhaps distressed, will begin blinking at a much faster rate. This can be a giveaway for someone who is lying, or it could simply be an indicator that this person is feeling uncomfortable. If you combine excessive blinking with other behaviors such as evasive eye contact, or too much of it, and sudden, almost jerking motions by the eyes only, and you might have a liar on your hands. In any event, your interlocutor may not be actually lying to you, but they would most certainly be hiding something from you. Thus, it is very important to keep an eye out for blinking. It is almost a dead giveaway indicator that something's up.

Another component of eye contact is squinting.

Most people squint when they can't see something clearly or there is something in their eyes. For example, when outdoors, it might be common to see folks squinting because it is too sunny or windy. In an indoor setting however, squinting can help you determine if your interlocutor is up to something.

When a person squints, they are engaging in a defensive position. How so? The main purpose of squinting is to help the eye focus on one particular object. As such, when a person is squinting in the middle of a conversation, it could signal that they are either focusing intently on what you are saying, or they might be taking on a defensive stance based on what they are saying. Consequently, a narrower field of vision may be an indication that your interlocutor is thinking about something else besides what you are currently speaking about.

When blinking and squinting are combined, you really need to pay attention to the context you are in. For example, it might simply be that you are dealing with someone who is having a hard time seeing. In such cases, you might be able to let your guard down. But if you couple these visual cues with other contextual clues, then you might be able to put together an accurate depiction of what your counterpart is actually thinking about.

Also, squinting is associated with evildoers. In most movies, you will find that the camera closes up on a villain's eyes in order to show them narrowing their eyes just a tad bit. This is a common device used to signal the audience that this particular character is up to no good.

That is why the same principle applies in usual visual communication. If you tend to squint too much, don't be surprised if people think you are mysterious or perhaps hiding what your true intentions really are.

One great way in which you can signal interest to your interlocutors is by opening your eyes wide. So, if narrowing your eyes is a sign that you might be up to something, then opening up your eyes can signal the opposite.

Here is a great trick when you are speaking with someone:

Whenever your counterpart says something that you genuinely find interesting, you can open your eyes up a little bit and nod. This signals to your interlocutor that you are listening to what they have to say. In addition, it tells them that you are interested in what they have to say.

This tip works really well when you are listening to your customers tell you about their needs. It makes customers feel validated as it indicates to them that what they have to say is important to you. By the same token, if you are in a regular conversation with a friend, relative or colleague, opening your eyes to emphasize that you are following their lead is a great way of building rapport.

Of course, you do want to be careful not to overdo it. For example, if you open up your eyes too big it may just look weird, or if you do it too often it might seem like you have something in your eyes. So, doing it once or twice every few minutes throughout a conversation can go a long way toward building that trust.

As you can see, "open" gestures are a common theme in this book. By being open with your body, you can help your interlocutors settle in and get comfortable around you. Likewise, if your gestures and mannerisms are "closed", then you can expect a similar reaction from your counterparts.

Ultimately, the most important thing takeaway from this chapter deals with maintaining the right amount of visual contact. While it is very hard to establish accurate parameters in terms of time, it is clear that a couple of second are more than enough to establish eye contact. While one or two seconds may not seem like a very long time, they actually are when you think about what it feels like to stare at someone directly in the eyes for an extended period of time For instance, ten seconds would qualify as an extended period of time.

76

Language And Psychology

Words To Make People Tick

In this chapter, we're going to discuss neuro-linguistic programming and how it applies to everything else we've covered in this book.

Believe it or not, we've already covered a few certain neuro-linguistic programming concepts.

What exactly is neuro-linguistic programming? We've made it this far into the book but haven't given it an exact definition just yet. Neuro- linguistic programming is the idea that you can use language to insert ideas into people's minds basically. In other words, you're subtly making suggestions that will eventually be accepted by a person's subconscious.

Through these techniques, you can slowly get people to accept whatever it is that you want them to do. Over a long period of time, people will come to see you as a primary influence, if you'd like to be. You can use the favors that you garnered with people to ask them for favors in turn.

Some of the ways that we've been using neuro-linguistic programming so far are setting up unique paradigms of honesty and outwardly charming personality traits. The combination of your general charm and your unique manner of speaking to people will make them see you as a trustworthy person.

Another way that we've discussed it is in the notion of taking yourself out of the equation and then framing the argument towards the thing that you want under the pretense of being objective. When you do this, you set things up such that the person starts to see you as impartial and objective. This is important because it programs people to value your opinion above the opinions of others because they see it as a more 'sound' idea than what others can offer.

So in the end, how can you take advantage of the concepts of neuro- linguistic programming to build your influence among people? There are a couple of different methods.

The first and foremost is to use it to establish an emotional connection between groups of people and yourself, or just one person and yourself. You need to start using terms like 'we' rather than 'I' to set up a subtle deference to either you or the group and a quiet sense of responsibility towards either you or the group. Don't completely replace 'I,' but do start referring to you and the person or people in question as a unit. This is an important part.

The second is to make yourself seem enigmatic. You do this by throwing people off-guard and coming off as someone who is very unique, as I've said before. Your goal isn't to ostracize or weird people out, though, so don't take it too far. What you ultimately want is for people to describe you positively, and that they see your personality and way of handling things as fundamentally distinct. There are some other ways to use language to subtly turn people against things or in favor of things. These work best either from a false-objective standpoint (like the detached standpoint that we talked about before) or from a position where they see you as an influential person. There's actually a deep connotation with positive and negative words, such that even using positive or negative words in relation to something when somebody cares about your opinion can create a situation where they innately start to connect those positive or negative words to those concepts. For example, if you were trying to present one college as good and one college as bad, you could use vaguely good terms and phrasing to define the first while using vaguely bad terms and phrasing to define the second.

If you're too overt in this approach, people will realize that you're trying to make a contrast or a comparison between the two subjects. Rather, you need to use subtle phrasing. The first college, for example, may be 'affordable,' 'have great programs,' or 'a solid foundation.' The second college may be 'out of the way' or 'a little plain,' or you may just be 'a little worried about how good a degree from this one will look.'

It's with the use of these subtle phrases that you can begin to slowly program somebody's opinions regarding certain topics. Enough of this over time, and you can start to dramatically shift somebody's opinion on something.

Another way that you can program someone's opinions is to actually overstep the thing you don't like. For example, if you were trying to make an argument against something, you could say something so erroneously good about the opposition that the person will start to see it as ironic in their own mind and slowly see through what you presented. This is a very subtle and difficult thing to pull off, but it can be very rewarding when you do it right.

Remember, words have great power. One of the most important things that you can do is learn how to use this power to bend things in your favor.

Creating A Magnetic Presence

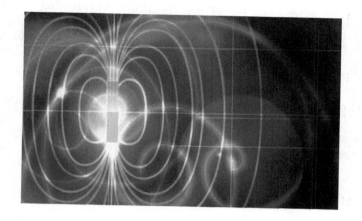

When you develop a magnetic presence, you become fascinating. You become mesmerizing. Other people cannot get enough of you. They look at you and want to

know more. People will like you and will feel drawn to you. They are more likely to want to help you or work with you in a business pursuit. A magnetic presence is how you get people to like you, trust you, and want to follow you. Having a presence that hooks people can get you very far in life, both in business and romance. You will make many friends and many contacts who want to be around you.

If you are shy or not naturally charismatic, you may believe that the idea of having a magnetic presence is a fantasy. But do you remember how earlier I said that you have innate abilities to do anything locked away inside yourself? You can be great and social, you just have some sort of blockage that is preventing you from being that way. Now you can use NLP to overcome that blockage and become a magnetic person. So stop thinking that you "can't" be social or magnetic in any way. You really can. You just need to unlock this ability within yourself. Where there is a will, there is a way.

Become More Charismatic

Charisma attracts and even hooks other people. For some, it is a natural trait. The only reason you may not possess charisma is because you have a mental block against being charismatic. It is surprising how the littlest things can make you seem magnetic and charismatic.

Part of becoming charismatic involves being very relaxed and calm. You can use NLP relaxation exercises to become more charismatic. Use breathing and progressive muscle relaxation to become more easygoing in public.

When you meet people, you want to make them feel special. This is part of charm. Beyond smiling and giving good eye contact and a firm handshake, you should always remember someone's name. An NLP memory trick can be helpful in this. When someone tells you his or her name, imagine it written in huge capital letters on a placard around his or her neck. Then always refer to him or her by name. This gesture of politeness will make people feel a connection with you. They are also disarmed whenever you use their name in an interview or when they are asking hard questions.

You can use more yes-oriented language. Ask questions that people are likely to say yes to, such as, "It has been a nice day, hasn't it?" or "It is very sunny today, isn't it?" When people say yes to you, they enter a more positive frame of mind.

<u>Become Sexy</u>

Your sexiness is rarely dependent on your looks. It is instead dependent on your personality and the allure that you exude. You can use NLP to become sexier without doing anything to change your appearance. Sexiness is largely based on confidence. Approaching people with a bold smile and a handshake is sexy in and of itself. But having high self-esteem is also attractive.

Often your low self-esteem is a paradigm that you have learned from childhood. But that does not mean that it is permanent. You can become more confident in yourself by believing that you are confident and that you are capable of anything. If this belief goes against your

natural paradigm, then envision confidence as a golden aura glowing around you. This aura makes you invincible.

Also, closely watch how people move physically. You can easily mirror their movements without being too obvious. Mirroring makes others feel more comfortable and attracted to you since people love those who are similar to them.

In addition, try to find things in common with people. When you match them in some way, they will like you more. A woman or man will feel more attracted to you if you share some of his or her interests in life.

Develop an Attractive Voice

What is an attractive voice to you? It is probably a voice that you cannot help but notice. It is voice that projects across a room. It is also deep for a man or sultry for a woman.

Now, imagine the power and the physical sensation of having this kind of voice. Imagine yourself speaking this way and projecting your voice across a room. Watch how it makes people stop and stare. In private, practice talking in this way. When you think you have it down, try it out in public. You can try it out in a strange place where no one knows you so that your friends and family don't wonder why you are talking differently all of a sudden.

Body Language Attraction

You can make yourself more attractive to others by how you posture your body. Your body language communicates many things that you are not saying. You may have a stiff posture because you are nervous, but other people will read into this as a sign that you do not like them. You can put people off and make people dislike you with your body language.

It is better to have a relaxed, inviting posture that makes others feel like you are approachable. Have your shoulder angled forward and your limbs dangling loosely. Smile. Don't hunch up in tension. Avoid fidgeting or shoving your hands into your pocket.

When someone is talking to you, avoid angling your feet away from them. Feet pointing away from a person or toward an exit suggest that you are not interested in the conversation and that you really just want to get away. Women especially are adept at reading body language and will find this kind of body language a turn-off.

The Time To Talk Is Now

One of the biggest obstacles to success when starting a new connection is getting those first few words out there. One thing that people have in common is that they want to know

what they are going to say before they actually open their mouths and say it. This is what leaves a lot of important conversations stalled before they start; if you can find a way around this obstacle, you are well on your way.One thing that is important to understand is that we generate language unconsciously. We choose our words and our grammar structures in unconscious parts of our mind; even if we consciously adopt a new persona, as if we are in a play or other dramatic capacity, after a while the use of language slips into an unconscious mode. Once you set a goal for your communication, your unconscious mind locks onto it and builds all of your language accordingly, even if you are not aware of the specifics of the construction process. Think back to the last time you talked to someone on the phone. It is as likely as not that you weren't consciously plotting the exact sequence of words that came out of your mouth. The precise structuring of your sentences likely happened in the unconscious recesses of your mind, rather than emerging as a conscious product. The key to developing some fluency with NLP language patterns works this way: first, you practice your general patterns until they have become a part of your unconscious practices. Then, you establish a goal for your communication before beginning to talk. If you have done these things in the right order, you will notice that the patterns emerge in a way that is spontaneous and automatic.

One barrier that people encounter at this point is that they just do not want to make a mistake or look ridiculous to others. So a good way to begin is to imagine that you are in an experimental laboratory. In this

lab, the usual customs about social interaction no longer apply. You could open your mouth and start singing show tunes, shouting what would in any other situation be considered obscenities, or whisper unintelligible gibberish, and no one will judge you. This takes you back to a point in time that resembles early childhood. When you were at that point in your life, you did not even know what failure meant. You made sounds as part of an experiment, figuring out how your vocal cords worked and how each different attempt yielded particular responses.The same process is true when it comes to mastering hypnotic language. You have to permit yourself the chance to make so-called "errors" in order to grow and learn as a communicator. The most important part of the process is to establish a goal for communication before you do anything else. This way, you teach your unconscious mind to generate phrases that will propel you toward the goal that you have established for yourself. If you do not select a specific target, you will end up at the target that has been bouncing around inside your subconscious the whole time. Everyone has targets lurking in their unconscious, and these goals can relate to just about anything. Here are some examples:

You may become aware of_when you_.

You may become aware of something, which means that you are assuming that this something is already in place, just waiting for you to figure out what the "when you" part is — in other words, the steps you have to go through in order to gain that awareness. An example would be developing a deeper sense of trance that would come when you turn your attention toward your inner self. Similarly, you might develop awareness of a new host of possibilities when you permit your unconscious mind to begin coming up with solutions. Also, you might gain awareness of a growing feeling of confidence as you put the NLP patterns to work for you over and over again.

Another example that I commonly use is this:

What will happen when you?

It's just a simple question. However, in order to find out exactly what happens, it is necessary for you to do it. For example, what happens when you visualize yourself living with the advantages of having made your way through this transformation? What will happen when you imagine having the ability to put all of these patterns to work without much in the way of effort?

This is a pattern that I use quite regularly to bring about powerful effects. To find out how patterns like this can be effective for you, several steps are necessary:

1. Read the entire text of the pattern and description out loud, etching it into your memory both visually and audibly.

2. Establish a communication goal. This could be to bring someone into a trance state, to help someone feel better, to speed up learning, or to bring about deep relaxation.

3. Begin reading just the pattern (the part that is in bold) out loud again. You don't yet know consciously what is going into the blanks, but you will see that the unconscious can fill them in just for you.

4. Permit yourself the liberty of stumbling a bit as you go through this the first couple of times. Enjoy the feeling that comes with improving with each attempt.

This form of hypnotic language can work wonders as you help people find your own way in these new forms of communication.

Take A Look Around

John Grinder said once that there are three primary obstacles in between you and a skill that you want to master. These three obstacles are a sense of hesitation, internal conversations and an excessive reliance on focal vision.

When it comes to mastering the principles of NLP, which requires you to put your ability to see the wider perspective on things and take action on the basics of instincts, these three factors can lead to a form of paralysis.

However, when you find ways to get past these hindrances, you are on the path to increasing your abilities exponentially. One of the fastest and most workable ways to get quick results is to look around yourself

— in other words, to put your peripheral vision to work.

A few years ago, I met a man who had spent two decades as a lion tamer, and he told me all about his line of work. One of the most important lessons I took from our conversation was that you have to take extreme care when you are working with lions so that you do not reinforce the wrong concepts.

When they are living with a circus, lions spend a lot of time simply listening and watching, which means they notice every little detail. They also notice patterns that even escape the notice of the trainers, because they are even paying more attention. If they see a pattern in reinforcement than the tamer overlooks, the lions will use those patterns for their own benefits. How do the lions notice so many things? It comes down to peripheral vision.

Focal vision is what you use to see things right in front of you. As you peruse this book, you are using focal vision to take in the words. While you spend the most time paying attention to this part of your visual field, it is a fairly small part of what you can actually see.

This part is terrific when it comes to helping you locate finer details. Most of us tend to rely mostly on the focal part of our vision; think of it as a direct line between the outside world and the conscious mind. Peripheral vision surrounds the focal vision area and expands in all directions. Peripheral vision is particularly good for picking up on movement. Think about peripheral vision as having a direct link to your unconscious.

Here's a demonstration. Focus on the "H" at the beginning of this paragraph. While you keep looking at it, allow your gaze to relax, and give yourself permission to feel awareness of the page's edges, and then let your awareness wander even further around the area of focal vision. Figure out how much you are able to perceive all over the paper, the desk and other areas well.

This area that you take in is your peripheral vision. If you use peripheral vision during a face to face conversation, you will glean much more information about your conversational partner – information that you may not otherwise have been able to gather in any other way.

You'll notice elements like nonverbal gestures, blinking rate, breathing rate and other useful metrics that can help you construct a degree of rapport. This also permits your unconscious self to join in the fun and for you to develop intuition about your conversational partner.

Here's another trick to try with peripheral vision. Sit in a position that is comfortable and relaxed while looking straight ahead. Imagine that your body has another set of eyes, even with your navel. Allow yourself to be cognizant of a sense of skin at your abdomen, and also pretend that you are looking out at the world through that pair of eyes.

The majority of people report that this expands the "visible" range of their peripheral vision. Of course, this range was always there, but you had to push to find it by stretching the area that you think you can see. If not, try this next tip.

Be seated in a position that is relaxed and comfortable, while looking ahead. Pretend that an orange is floating just above and to the rear of your head.

Maintaining this pretense should help you open up your area of peripheral vision. As a result, when this gaze widens and relaxes, you should be able to see more. The best way to help your gaze to move into peripheral vision is through practice. The more you work on this, the easier it will be for you to use your peripheral vision in a natural way.

Now try slipping into peripheral vision when you're in a face to face conversation with someone. Make mental notes of the things you are now aware of that you did not notice before.

As your comfort level with peripheral vision in the middle of different social situations grows, you will be amazed at the things that you see that simply escaped your notice before.

Improving Communication Skills

Communication is of extreme importance and it is compulsory that you be able to speak with others freely and openly. You have to drive across a point such that the other person

understands it in the same context as you. Having problems communicating can lead to all types of issues, which can be both mental and physical in nature. So, you have to make the effort of improving your skills and using it to your advantage. Let us now look at things that you can do to improve your communication.

Body Language

The very first thing to concentrate on is your body language. Try to have an open body language as opposed to a closed one. This means that you keep your hands and legs free instead of folding them. Also avoid placing your hands inside your pockets. Keep them free and don't remain fidgety. All these serve as distractions and you might not be able to drive across the point properly. If you are sitting and having a conversation, then don't cross your legs. Have your hands on the seat handles and remain steady? Have a pleasant expression on your face and remain as calm and collected as possible.

No Fillers

It is a very annoying habit to use fillers in your conversation. This includes using "umm" or "uhh" in between your sentences. These will not only annoy the other person but also you yourself! Try to speak normally and maintain a consistent tone. If you are not getting a word,

then instead of using a filler word, keep quiet and try to recall the word. If it is still not coming to your mind then ask the other person for the word. That way, you can keep the conversation going and keep it interesting.

No Cellphones!

Do not use cell phones while having conversations. They are possibly the worst distractions. You will end up saying something wrong or something beside the main point. Even if the phone rings, ask for a second to put it on silent and then go back to the conversation.

Empathy

Empathy is an important quality to possess while talking to someone. It refers to connecting with the other person and understanding what they are going through. Many times, even if we are not in the mood to listen to someone, we have to remain patient and empathetic. Don't rush the person or act like you are disinterested.

You will come across as being extremely rude. Instead, focus on the person and the issue. You will be able to help them out and save both your time and theirs. You will feel good for having helped someone and find a good friend in the person.

Language

It is important that you focus on your language and make use of simple words as much as possible. If there is an easier way to express something then choose that over something complex. You will be able to save on both time and effort by doing so.

If you don't have knowledge of the local language then try to make best use of your limbs to express yourself.

Eye Contact

Maintaining consistent eye contact with the other person is extremely important. When you are addressing someone, look them in the eye while speaking with them and don't look here and there. Remain focused on the person and try to understand their body language. If you are not comfortable looking into their eyes then it is a trick to stare at the tip of their nose as that will make them think you are looking at their eyes.

No Giggling

Don't giggle when you are talking to someone or after you walk away from them. It can be misconstrued, and the person will think that you are laughing at them. If you wish to laugh, then quickly explain why you did so to avoid misunderstandings.

Questions

It is important to ask the person questions and also answer them. This will keep it as interactive as possible. If you have a do8bt then ask immediately or keep it in your mind and then ask everything together. Try to remain as open to a question and answer session has an interactive conversation as much as possible. Information

While speaking, listen carefully and gather as much information as you can when you are listening to someone. It should literally be like a doctor listening to a patient and picking up important points. You can also have a book and pen handy to write all the questions and then ask them one by one. Apart from questions, you must also write any information that you pick up from the conversation and use it at a later time.

Listening

Make use of something known as "mindful listening" when having a serious conversation with another person. This refers to keenly listening to whatever they have to say and cutting all the noise out. It will help you pick up things that you might not be able to pick up if you are not listening using this technique.

Trivia

Although it is fine to speak trivial things, you should know when to and when not to bring it up. So, if you are having a serious discussion with someone then doesn't unnecessarily trivialize it by speaking of things that are not relevant. Go straight to the point and once done, you can speak on trivial matters.

Intentions

Never jump the gun and misjudge someone's intentions. You might think that they are trying to show you down or have ill intentions for you but the reality might be just the opposite. So don't have conversations hoping for the worst and try to remain as positive while speaking to others as possible.

These are the different things that you can do to improve your communication skills.

Examples of Hypnotic Language Patterns You Can Use Today!

Thanks for bearing with me through the background information about presuppositions and Hypnotic Language Patterns. Now that we've covered everything you need to

know, let's dive right in with our examples!

Many of these examples will be sales-focused, but you'll soon be able to see how easy it is to fit these examples into almost any situation you can think of!

Quantifiers

Examples of Quantifiers: All, each, every, some, many, none

Quantifiers are used to quantify some vague amount of something; the audience is left to conclude the exact amount themselves. Quantifiers make use of presuppositions by implying that the thing already exists.

1.) Many of my customers love my product because it's made of real oak.

Notice how the focus is on X (Made of real oak) instead of "my customers".

So this vague "group of customers" is accepted as a pre-supposition by the audience's subconscious. People reading or listening will subconsciously accept that you have a large customer base. We use our subconscious to automatically fill quantifiers in with something that's

meaningful to us, which is why they're so powerful. The audience will often imagine people like themselves being a part of your customer base, which is exactly what you want!

2.) Some of my customers even use my product to decorate their coffee table.

3.) Each one of my customers has found many different uses for my product.

Examples 2 and 3 both presuppose that the customer base is large and undefined. Notice how example 3 also presupposes that the product is useful. Since there are "many different uses" for the product, logically, the product must have at least one use. Our subconscious accepts that the product fulfills its intended use and is in fact useful.

4.) Few of my customers haven't found several uses for my product.

This example is more complex because it's in the negative. This is a very hypnotic phrase, and just fuzzes right into the reader's brain. The sentence presupposes that the customer base is large, and the audience will start to imagine all of the different uses for your product other than the main, obvious use. This is extremely powerful, because each person will imagine something different- something that's useful and meaningful to them. Perfect!

Presupposing Social Proof

Using social proof is a great way to bolster the message you're trying to get across to your audience. People like to fit in, and don't like to feel like outliers. They'd be hesitant to be the first one to do something, but when they realize that plenty of others have already done it, they're much more likely to take action!

Here's a great way to assume social proof and authority: (noun phrase) + which/who/that

People/experts (which/who/that) (use/know) 5.) Experts who use my product are very happy.

What kind of experts? Experts in what? Each person will imagine something different. Their subconscious will fill in the blank with something meaningful to them; something that will, in their eyes, qualify the sentence to be true.

6.) People who use my product love it.

Again, notice how vague this is. What kind of people? Who knows! Your audience will fill in the blank with people like them, which is exactly what we want. This is a very hypnotic phrase, because they'll see themselves in the future as one of these "people" loving your product.

Borrowing Authority

Borrowing authority is another example of presupposing social proof. Typically, it's best to use an authority figure, or a group of people that your audience will know of and trust. Your audience's subconscious will then validate your claim as true.

7.) Fortune 500 CEOs who use fountain pens prefer oak fountain pens like mine.

Notice what you're doing here: you're creating an association between your product to the idea of Fortune 500 CEOs. Each person will have a different idea of what a Fortune 500 CEO is like, and it'll be something powerful and meaningful to them.

Also, it's important to notice that you're not being untruthful. While you're creating a subconscious link between Fortune 500 CEOs to your product, you're not saying explicitly that Fortune 500 CEOs use your product. We never want to be dishonest when using Hypnotic Language Patterns.You're just saying that Fortune 500 CEOs use a product similar to yours, and your readers will fill in the blanks and make the link.

8.) Scientists who use my fountain pens prefer heavy ones like mine, because they're more stable.

Again, audience will be creating subconscious links between your product and this vague group of "scientists". When your customer buys the product, they'll actually tell themselves that they're buying the product because scientists use this particular product. They'll convince themselves that it's backed by science, and that that's why they're making the purchase.

Time Clauses

Examples of time clauses: before, after, during, since

Time clauses are a great way to "assume the close". The presupposition is that your audience will buy or take the action you want them to take—there's no question that they're going to buy. Time clauses are very hypnotic, because they get people to project into the future, to a point when they've already taken the action you want them to take.

9.) After you buy my fountain pen, you'll notice how easy it is to use. Note that the sentence presupposes that your product is easy to use.

Beyond that, though, using the time clause "after" presupposes that the event "buy" has already taken place. This is very hypnotic, because

your audience projects themselves into the future having already bought the product.

10.) Before you buy my fountain pen, be sure you really want the amazing benefits. It's not for everyone.

Here, you're making the focus whether or not they want the benefits of your product, thus it's presupposed that the product has amazing benefits. Note the time clause, "before". You're also explicitly putting them in control, by telling them it's not for everyone, and to be sure they really want the amazing benefits before they buy it.

This is a fantastic Hypnotic Language Pattern to use, because your message is very clearly validated both on the subconscious and conscious levels.

11.) Since you're reading this, you're already aware of the amazing value this product has.

We's using the time clause "since"; let's break down this sentence and see why it works. "Since you're reading this"— they are reading it, so what you're going to say must be true. "You're already aware of how much value this product has". Again, that's assumed to be true, but look what happens if they disagree!

Even if they think, "no, I'm not already aware of how much value it has", they presuppose that the product has value, so they really are already aware that the product has value. This is another very powerful hypnotic loop you can use!

<u>Comparative Words</u>

Examples of comparative words: more, less, better, cheaper

Using comparative language in your message works a lot like a "cause and effect" sentence, or a "because" sentence. We'll cover those later, and you'll see the similarities.

12.) The longer that people stay on my email list, the more valuable information they learn.

This sentence presupposes that there are lots of people on the email list. It also presupposes that they have been there for a long time, they trust you, and they've chosen to stay for a long time rather than leave. This all presupposes that you're established and trustworthy, and that you must be delivering the value that you claim to be.

13.) The sooner you download your product, the sooner you'll be enjoying the proven benefits.

Not only does this sentence presuppose that your audience will download your product, but also it presupposes that your product has proven benefits. It doesn't say how they're proven explicitly, so the reader will fill that in with whatever is most applicable to them.

14.) If you can find a cheaper product that can deliver more value, I'll double your money back.

Using "if" presupposes that what follows might not be true. This creates doubt that the reader can find a cheaper product that delivers more value—a product like that might not even exist. Notice how this sentence also presupposes that your product is cheap, and also delivers value.

By using "double your money back", you're presupposes they've already purchased the product and spent the money.

This is very hypnotic, because it causes the reader to project into the future when they've already purchased your product, and have experienced its value.

Repetitive Words

Example of Repetitive Words: again, either, also, back

Repetitive words are great, because any time you use one, the reader or listener will subconsciously imagine something happening twice, which reinforces the idea you're trying to drive home.

15.) Many of my customers keep coming back again and again.

This sentence has a lot going on: it presupposes you have lots of customers, and that they keep coming back again and again. It doesn't explicitly say why, but your audience will assume that there must be some good reason why they're coming back again and again. It can't be to get a refund, since that would only be coming back once. There must be some sort of value that they're receiving from your product.

16.) Authorities have also found that this product delivers a second benefit.

Authorities? Who knows who they are. You don't say, but your readers will imagine something that's meaningful to them; something that will give your product authority in their mind. Using "also found" presupposes that these "authorities" have already found some kind of first benefit. With all of these things, the reader's subconscious fills in the blank with their own imagination and accepts these presuppositions as true.

17.) You can either shop around and find a more expensive product, or you can buy today and never be worried again.

So, this pre-supposes that your product is the cheapest out there today—by shopping around, they'll only find a more expensive product. You're also presupposing that when they buy today their problems will be over. This implies that those more expensive products won't even solve their problems, so they can either go shopping around and waste all that time to not solve their problem, or they can buy your product today and get rid of their problem now.

<u>Qualifiers</u>

Examples of Qualifiers: only, except, just, even

Qualifiers are great for making up imaginary boundaries and then breaking them, which makes whatever you're saying seem even more impactful

18.) You only need to pay once, since there is no monthly fee.

With most things that you buy, you only need to pay once. But this makes it seem like that's an added benefit.

CONCLUSION

Thank you for reading all this book!

Neuro Linguistic Programming is a hugely successful program because it resonates with a wide swath of thinking and behavior patterns. It will, no doubt, have an impact on you.

To what degree that impact is, depends on how far you pursue it and how receptive you are to 'just another self-help program'.

Let me tell you that this is a very simple program at the early stages and can get daunting especially for some of us who are really wired differently and find that psychobabble is not real. That's the main reason I included the science behind the brain. The evidence for the scientific facts of the brain, neuroplasticity and how you are who you are is incontrovertible.

Your beliefs are something that you don't realize, and you should take the time to take stock of them. There might be something that is tripping you up that you don't fully comprehend. It could be a simple matter and easily fixed, but because you are not aware of it, it is tripping you up.

You have already taken a step towards your improvement.
Best wishes!